WHAT IS

TECHNOLOGY?

The who, where, why, and how!

Written by Frances Du...

Illustrated by The Boy Fitz Hammond

FOR YOUNG READERS

Text and illustrations copyright © 2023 by b small publishing ltd. First Racehorse for Young Readers Edition 2023. 10 9 8 7 6 5 4 3 2 1 Print ISBN: 978-1-63158-714-6 Ebook ISBN: 978-1-63158-724-5

Publisher: Sam Hutchinson • Art Director: Vicky Barker • Designer: Karen Hood • Printed in Malaysia

CONTENTS

TOOLS THAT ROCK

The Stone Age is the name for the period of history from around 3.3 million years ago to 3,300 BC, when early humans and other **hominids** used rocks and stones as tools. The first stone tools were those that could be picked up and immediately used to crush, grind, or be thrown as weapons.

The earliest examples of manufactured stone tools are known as Oldowan tools. These were simple broken stones that could be used for chopping, crushing, grinding, and preparing animal skins. It is thought that these were created by *Homo habilis* and *Australopithecus*.

The tools became more advanced over time. Aechulean tools were flaked on both sides to create sharper edges. These included hand-axes, arrowheads, knives, spearheads, and **adzes**. They were made by *Homo erectus* and *Homo heidelbergensis* and could be used for hunting, preparing food, and making things.

Early stone age woman cleaning an animal skin with stone tools

Homo sapien wielding a knapped axe

---

c. 3.3 million – 300,000 years ago

Early Stone Age
Lower Palaeolithic

Early hominids, including *Homo habilis* and *Homo erectus*.

Tools for all types of tasks were made from stones.

300,000 – 40,000 years ago

Middle Stone Age
Middle Palaeolithic

Homo sapiens and Neanderthals developed techniques to make the stones into better tools.

3,300 BC

The Stone Age ends and the Bronze Age begins.

These tools are evidence of human evolution. They show how our ancient ancestors lived, hunted, and interacted with their environment.

From around 250,000 years ago *Homo sapiens* and *Neanderthals* knapped longer blades for cutting and made tiny blades called microliths that were inserted into handles. It is during this period that early cave paintings were made.

MODERN STONE TOOLS

Obsidian is a type of igneous rock that is formed when the lava from a volcano cools very quickly. It was used in the Stone Age to produce very sharp blades. Today, obsidian blades are sharper than steel but they are very brittle and can break easily. Obsidian scalpel blades are sometimes used in surgery but they are too fragile for common use.

obsidian

WHAT IS KNAPPING?

Knapping is the process of creating stone tools by striking a large stone, the core, with a hammerstone in order to chip off flakes. These flakes could then be knapped further to create the specific shape that was required. This method was used during the Stone Age to make all kinds of sharp-edged tools, often from a kind of stone called flint.

TAKE IT FURTHER

The Iron Age ended when the Bronze Age began. We call it the Bronze Age because there is evidence of the creation and use of bronze in the archaeology from that time.

What difference do you think this new material made to the lives of the people who lived then?

HOT OFF THE PRESS

About 600 years ago, German inventor Johannes Gutenberg created a printing press that was faster and more powerful than other machines at the time. Previous inventions inspired Gutenberg to perfect his press. These incuded **moveable type** from China, papermaking techniques from China brought to Europe by the Arab influence in Spain, durable ink from Flemish painters, and traditional wine and olive wooden presses from Roman times.

Before Gutenberg's press, monks created books by hand. This new printing press was much faster! Suddenly, it was possible to spread information far and wide.

If printing technology already existed, what did Gutenberg do differently and why did his press have such a big impact on history?

Chinese writing uses many thousands of different characters but the Latin alphabet, most widely used in books in Europe at the time, demanded just over 50 different pieces of moveable type, including upper- and lower-case letters and numerals. Gutenberg's passion for **metallurgy** resulted in the creation of a **lead alloy** that could melt and set quickly, allowing him to produce lots of pieces of very durable type.

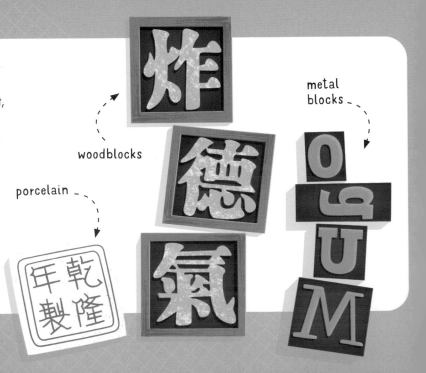

metal blocks

woodblocks

porcelain

Bi Sheng
Hubei, China

Bi Shing, a Chinese engineer, made Chinese characters from porcelain. Printers pressed ink on to paper with them. This was called moveable type.

Johann Gutenberg
Mainz, Germany

Johannes Gutenberg left Mainz for Strasbourg, now in France. Inspired by his desire to create the perfect machine, Gutenberg worked on his printing press in secret.

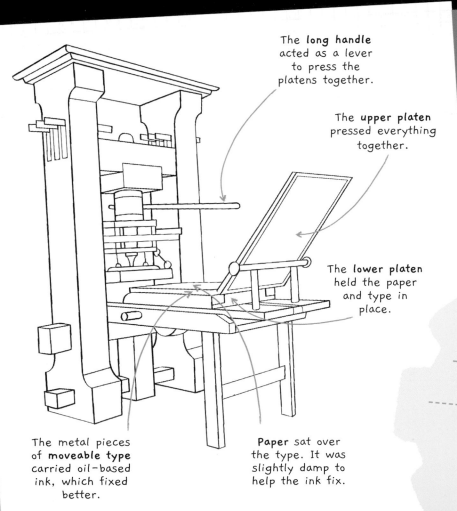

The **long handle** acted as a lever to press the platens together.

The **upper platen** pressed everything together.

The **lower platen** held the paper and type in place.

The metal pieces of **moveable type** carried oil-based ink, which fixed better.

Paper sat over the type. It was slightly damp to help the ink fix.

THE GUTENBERG PRESS

This new machine allowed a printer to transfer lettering from the metal type to paper using ink to create a crisp, sharp, high-quality image. When up and running, the press could produce up to 250 pages an hour.

TAKE IT FURTHER

Full name:
Johann Gensfleisch zur Laden zum Gutenberg!

- - - - - - - - - - - - - - - - - - -

The Gutenberg Project is a digital library of over 60,000 copyright-free books.

- - - - - - - - - - - - - - - - - - -

Information is a powerful tool. How would Gutenberg's press change things for someone living in a village or town who previously had no power or access to information? How might wealthy people use the press to get what they want?

PAINTING WITH LIGHT

In 1839 a French physicist named Louis Daguerre announced that he had invented a way of using chemicals to capture an image on a silver-plated sheet of copper. He called it the daguerreotype. Daguerre's process exposed these sheets to light, and used iodine and mercury to fix the image so that it didn't fade. Anyone who wanted their photograph taken had to remain completely still for 20 minutes!

The word photography comes from the Greek words *fos* which means "light" and *grafo* which means "to write."

c. AD 965 - AD 1040

Ibn al-Haytham
Cairo, Egypt

Ibn al-Haytham carried out optical experiments by projecting an image on to a screen through a hole in the wall.

1787 - 1851

Louis Daguerre
France

Daguerre invented the first practical and commercially available photographic process.

CAMERA OBSCURA

The principles behind using light to create an image had been around for hundreds of years before the invention of the daguerreotype. Around 400 BC the Chinese philosopher Mozi observed that when light from an object passed through a tiny hole it projected an inverted (upside-down) image of the original object. This was later called the *camera obscura* ("dark chamber") and in the nineteenth century this idea was used to create the first pinhole camera.

pinhole camera

HOW DOES A PINHOLE CAMERA WORK?

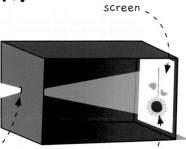

screen

box

light rays

pin hole

upside-down image

A pinhole camera is a box with a small hole in one side. When light bounces off an object and passes through the hole in the camera it forms an image of that object on the back of the box.

In modern cameras the pinhole is replaced by a lens which can allow in much more light.

TAKE IT FURTHER

Build a pinhole camera!

Cut a square opening on one side of a cardboard box and tape a piece of tissue paper over the top. Use a pin to make a tiny hole on the opposite side. Cover yourself and the back of the camera with a blanket. Point the pinhole towards an object. When you look at the tissue paper you should see the inverted object appear.

1859 – 1939

Frank A. Brownell
Rochester, New York, USA

While working for the Kodak company in 1900, Brownell invented the Brownie camera. This was a small and affordable camera that became very popular with amateur photographers.

2000

Samsung released the first mobile phone with an in-built camera.

THE MAGIC OF MAKING MUSIC

Aerophones are instruments that use **vibrating** air to make sound. There are lots of different types of aerophones, from wind instruments such as flutes and clarinets to brass instruments like trumpets and saxophones.

The earliest known musical instruments are simple flutes made from swan bones and woolly mammoth ivory. They had finger holes that the musician would use to alter the sound. These instruments were found in a cave in southern Germany and are around 42,000 years old.

Flutes and trumpets became part of cultures all over the world. At first, they were mostly made from natural materials: bone, horns, wood, bamboo, or even shells. The interior spiral shape of the conch shell meant that it was used as a trumpet across the Americas, India, China, Oceania, and Europe. But ornate metal trumpets were found in the burial chamber of Egyptian Pharoah Tutankhamun who died in 1323 BC.

Playing a conch shell

HOW DOES AN AEROPHONE WORK?

The simplest aerophone is a tube which can be blown into. The addition of holes into the side of the tube means that a player can use their fingers to cover them and alter the notes. The shape and length of the tube also affects the noise that the aerophone makes.

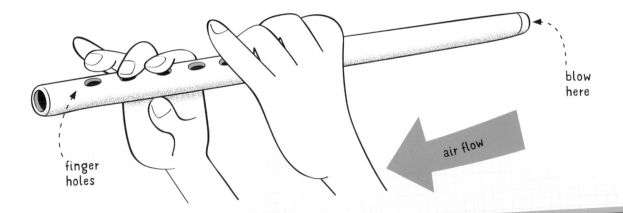

blow here

air flow

finger holes

Some aerophones use keys to help the player cover holes that are difficult to reach with one pair of hands. This **mechanism** was first invented for the flute by Theobald Boehm in the nineteenth century. Over time, new materials meant that new instruments were created in different shapes, including the clarinet, oboe, recorder, accordion, trombone, tuba, and the saxophone.

TAKE IT FURTHER

New musical instruments are being invented all the time. In 2017 Yamaha released the Venova which is a cross between a saxophone and a recorder.

Can you invent a new instrument or think of a way to change an old one?

40,000 BC

Modern-day Germany

Early modern humans made flutes from animal bones.

1324 BC

Thebes, Egypt

Beautiful instruments, such as ceremonial trumpets, were made of metal.

1794 – 1881

Theobald Boehm
Munich, Germany

Boehm was a musician who used his skills as a goldsmith to modernize the flute and the Boehm-system is still in use today.

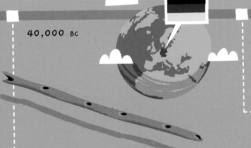

FUN FACT A 43,000-year-old bone with holes was found in Slovenia in 1995 but there is a lot of debate about whether it was an instrument or if the holes were made by animal teeth.

TINY TECHNOLOGY

In the first half of the twentieth century, electronic devices such as televisions, radios, and computers contained vacuum tubes that controlled the flow of the electric current. These were big, heavy, expensive, and fragile. In 1947, a team of physicists including John Bardeen invented a smaller and more efficient way to control the electric current, called a **transistor**.

- - - → a vacuum tube

a transistor - - - →

Old television sets had big vacuum tubes inside them

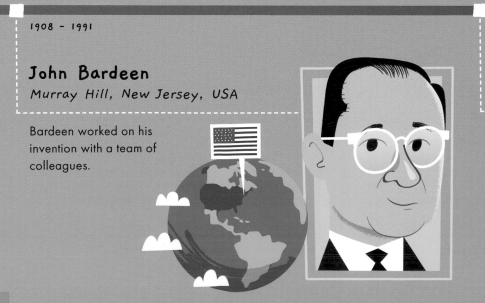

1908 – 1991

John Bardeen
Murray Hill, New Jersey, USA

Bardeen worked on his invention with a team of colleagues.

1923 – 2005

Jack Kilby
Dallas, USA

Kilby created the integrated circuit when he combined very small electronic components on to a piece of material that conducts electricity in certain situations (a **semiconductor**). This was the first microchip.

first microchip

In 1958, Jack Kilby made the technology even smaller when he invented the integrated circuit, also known as the **microchip**. The microchip contains a lot of technology, including transistors, in a very small space and meant that the machines that used them could become smaller too.

OUT OF THIS WORLD

These tiny and powerful microchips meant that NASA's Apollo Guidance Computer could be small and light enough to be installed on spacecrafts. They were part of the vehicles that went to the Moon.

The success of the space program meant that demand for microchips grew. Today they can be found in mobile phones, smartwatches, robots, cars, and even toasters. Microchips with information are often implanted under the skin of pets so that their owners can find them if they ever get lost.

FUN FACT The engineer Gordon Moore said in 1965 that the number of transistors on a microchip would double every year. Today microchips contain billions of transistors.

TAKE IT FURTHER

Some people have suggested that humans could carry information in chips under their own skin. This could enable them to open doors or make payments with a wave of their hand.

- - - - - - - - - - - - - - - - - -

What do you think about the possibilities for microchips?

COMPUTER COMMUNICATION

In 1962, an American scientist named Joseph Carl Robnett Licklider came up with the idea for an "Intergalactic Computer Network" that allowed computers to communicate with each other. This inspired his colleagues at the US Department of Defence Advanced Research Projects Agency (ARPA) to invent the ARPANET. It used a technology called **packet-switching** to break down messages into smaller parts and send them through telephone lines where they would reach their destination and be rebuilt. The first message was sent between computers at two different universities in California in 1969.

It was supposed to send the word "LOGIN," but the network crashed after the first two letters.

In the beginning, only a few computers could use the ARPANET but, during the 1970s, new **protocols** were written to create a massive "inter-network" link that connected computers all over the world. It was nicknamed the "internet."

FUN FACT The Internet of Things refers to the growing number of everyday devices such as fridges, washing machines and lightbulbs that can connect to the internet.

During the Second World War, an inventor named Hedy Lamarr created a way to transmit radio signals across a wide range of frequencies. This **spread spectrum** technology reduced interference and made it difficult to jam or intercept signals. It became the basis for the wireless technology known as Wi-Fi that now gives us access to the internet no matter where we are.

Joseph Carl Robnett Licklider
Arlington, Virginia, USA

At a time when computer technology was growing quickly, Licklider came up with the idea that computers should be able to share information remotely.

Hedy Lamarr
Hollywood, California, USA

Lamarr worked on her invention at the same time as being a

Tim Berners-Lee
Geneva, Switzerland

Berners-Lee invented the World Wide Web. He released the source code for free and made the web accessible to everyone.

WHAT IS THE WORLD WIDE WEB?

When the internet first started, it was mostly used for sending emails and data files between computers. However, in 1989, a man named Tim Berners-Lee came up with the idea of using it as a place to store information that all internet users could access. He called it "Mesh" but changed the name to the "World Wide Web" and the first web page was created in 1991.

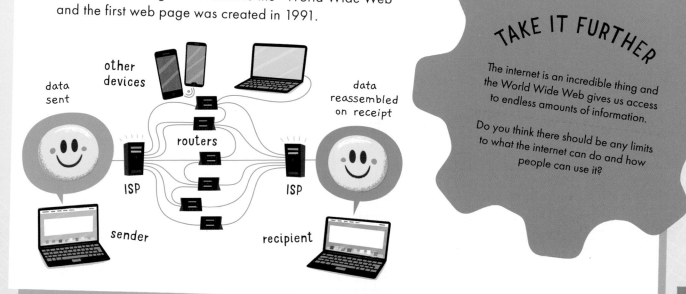

data sent

other devices

data reassembled on receipt

routers

ISP

ISP

sender

recipient

TAKE IT FURTHER

The internet is an incredible thing and the World Wide Web gives us access to endless amounts of information.

Do you think there should be any limits to what the internet can do and how people can use it?

POETRY IN MOTION

The wheel is an incredibly popular piece of engineering. Its origins are very mysterious but **archaeological evidence** shows a stone potter's wheel was used in Mesopotamia in around 3,500 BC. After that date, there is evidence of preserved wheel tracks, pictures of wheeled vehicles and toys with wheels across Asia, the Middle East, and Eastern Europe.

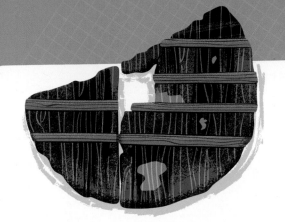

potter's wheel

The oldest surviving wooden wheel was discovered in Slovenia and is from around 3,000 BC. The first wheels were large and heavy solid discs of wood, eventually made lighter by the invention of **spokes** in around 2,000 BC. They were first used on horse-drawn chariots along the **Eurasian Steppe** before finding their way into Asia and Europe. These new wheels were so light and fast that chariot racing became a popular sport in parts of the ancient world.

c. 3,500 BC

Potter's wheel
Mesopotamia (modern-day Iraq)

Horizontal wheels were first used to turn clay as it was shaped into pottery.

c. 2,000 BC

Chariot Wheels
Ural Mountains, Eurasian Steppe (modern-day Russia)

Heavy wooden wheels were hollowed out to make spokes that connected the outer and inner edges.

Early tyres were made from leather and in around 1000 AD wheels were given iron **rims** to make them stronger. A very significant technological development arrived in 1846 when Robert William Thompson filled a hollow strip of **vulcanized** rubber with air and invented the first **pneumatic** tyre.

WHAT IS A WHEEL?

A wheel is a circular object that turns on an axle. It is used to make vehicles or parts of machinery move.

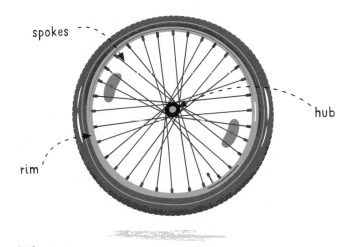

spokes

hub

rim

Wheels have lots of different uses and include spinning wheels, water wheels, steering wheels, and even the gears inside a clock are a type of wheel. Before the wheel was invented, the sled was an important method for transporting heavy items. Sleds carried heavy stones to build the pyramids, and sleds are still important today on terrains such ice and snow.

1822 – 1873

Robert William Thompson
London, England

Thompson used inflated rubber to create the kind of tire used today.

TAKE IT FURTHER

Can you improve on the wheel?

Can you think of new ways to use a wheel?

Are there any tasks that you think wheels would not help with?

MAGNETIC DIRECTION

Early travelers navigated the world using landmarks, the Sun and the stars. The compass was the first navigational tool but nobody today knows who invented it. In the eleventh century, the Chinese scientist Shen Kuo described how a **magnetized** needle suspended from a piece of silk would align itself with north and south. Before this, in China, the lodestone used to magnetize the needle was used for fortune telling and **feng shui**, not navigation, as it would point in a certain direction when left to spin on its own.

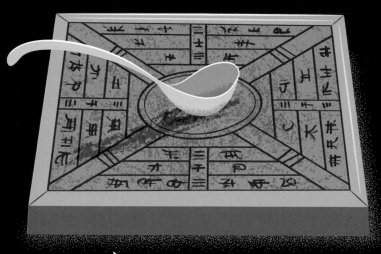

--- Chinese feng shui lodestone

This simple invention became widely used and, by around the year 1300 AD, the needle was suspended in a box above a compass rose that showed the cardinal points: north, south, east, and west.

box compass

HOW DOES A COMPASS WORK?

A compass is a navigational tool that uses a magnetized needle which lines up with the Earth's **Magnetic North Pole**. Magnetism was discussed by the ancient Greeks but the English physicist William Gilbert proposed, in 1600, that magnets point north because the Earth's core contains iron.

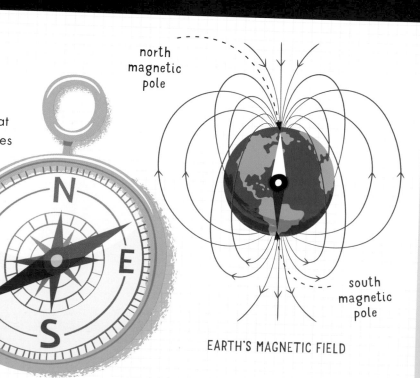

north magnetic pole

south magnetic pole

EARTH'S MAGNETIC FIELD

1031 – 1095

Shen Kuo
China

Shen Kuo was a Chinese scientist who wrote a book of essays that covered different scientific observations.

1930 –

Gladys West
Dahlgren, Virginia, USA

West developed a computer program that used satellites to create navigation systems. Cars, planes and ships now use this to find their way to their destinations.

WHAT IS GPS?

In the early 1960s, Gladys West worked at an American naval base. She used satellites to measure the shape of the Earth and programmed a computer to work out an extremely accurate **geodetic** model of the planet. Her work became the basis of the satellite navigation system known as Global Positioning System (GPS). Today there are several other Global Navigation Satellite systems including Galileo, GLONASS, and BeiDou.

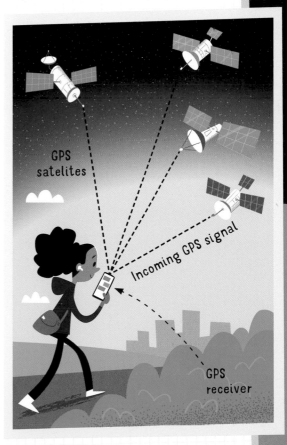

GPS satelites

Incoming GPS signal

GPS receiver

TAKE IT FURTHER

Before compasses were invented, travelers used the stars and the Sun to find their way. The Sun rises in the east and sets in the west. Can you use this to identify the cardinal directions of the compass from where you are?

At night, can you find Polaris, or the North Star?

A LIGHTBULB MOMENT

For thousands of years, humans used torches, oil lamps, candles, and lanterns to light rooms and streets. This finally changed at the end of the eighteenth century when gas lamps were invented but it was the power of electricity that completely transformed the way the world could be illuminated. The very first electric light was invented by Humphrey Davey in 1802. He passed an electric current through a platinum **filament** and made it glow. His invention wasn't very practical, but many more inventors worked on their own versions of this **incandescent light**.

Davy's first electric light

1778 – 1829

Humphrey Davy
Bristol, England

Davy's inventions led to the modern lightbulb.

1828 – 1914

Joseph Swan
Gateshead, England

Swan created a practical device that could be used safely inside homes and public buildings.

1902 – 1942

Oleg Losev
Nizhny Novgorod, Russia

While experimenting with semiconductors, Oleg Losev invented the first LED light.

In 1850, the British scientist Joseph Swan enclosed the filament inside a glass bulb. He used vacuum technology to remove the air from the bulb as oxygen would make the filament break apart. Swan continued his experiments and, in 1881, he started his own company to manufacture lightbulbs. The American inventor Thomas Edison had created his own version of the lightbulb just after Swan and the two men combined their companies to light homes and buildings all over Europe and America.

Thomas Edison's lightbulb

HOW A LIGHTBULB WORKS

When electricity passes through the filament of a lightbulb it causes it to glow. The filament in modern lightbulbs is a metal called tungsten.

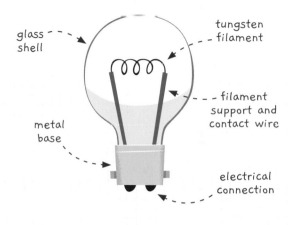

glass shell

tungsten filament

filament support and contact wire

metal base

electrical connection

The first public building in the world to be fully lit by electric lighting was the Savoy Theatre in London.

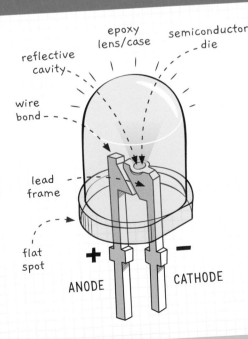

reflective cavity

epoxy lens/case

semiconductor die

wire bond

lead frame

flat spot

+ ANODE

− CATHODE

LIGHTING THE FUTURE

An LED (light emitting diode) is a tiny lightbulb without a filament. It creates light when an electric current passes through a **diode**. Russian scientist, Oleg Losev, created these in 1927. They are far more energy efficient and long-lasting than incandescent lightbulbs and are now a popular form of lighting.

TAKE IT FURTHER

Why do you think electric light was an important invention?

What do you think happened before artificial light?

PACKS OF POWER

In 1800, Luigo Galvani saw the muscles of a **dissected** frog move when he prodded them with two different pieces of metal. Galvani thought that the reaction came from the **tissue** of the animal, but his friend Alessandro Volta believed it was caused by the different metals and the liquid on the frog's legs. To test his idea, Volta placed cardboard soaked in salt water between stacked disks of copper and zinc. When the two types of metal were connected, the pile of disks created a steady electric current. The invention became known as the "voltaic pile," or the first electric battery.

Luigo Galvani's dissected frog experiment

HOW DOES A VOLTAIC PILE WORK?

A voltaic pile, as with other batteries, contains **chemical energy** that can become **electrical energy**. The first batteries were made of a liquid substance called an electrolyte stacked together with positive and negative metal **electrodes**. The electrolyte reacted with the positive electrode to create **electrons**. The negative electrode attracted those electrons, allowing the electrons to flow and creating an electrical current.

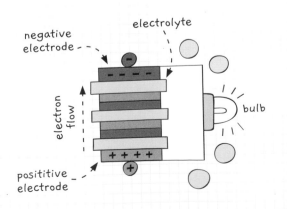

negative electrode

electrolyte

electron flow

bulb

posititive electrode

1745 – 1827

Alessandro Volta
Italy

A "volt" is now the word for a unit of electric potential.

POWERING INTO THE FUTURE

Following Volta's invention, many scientists improved upon his idea and the battery became a practical and convenient source of power. In the 1990s, research on lithium led Akira Yoshino to create the first lithium-ion battery. These rechargeable energy packs can be found in mobile phones, games consoles, and modern electric cars.

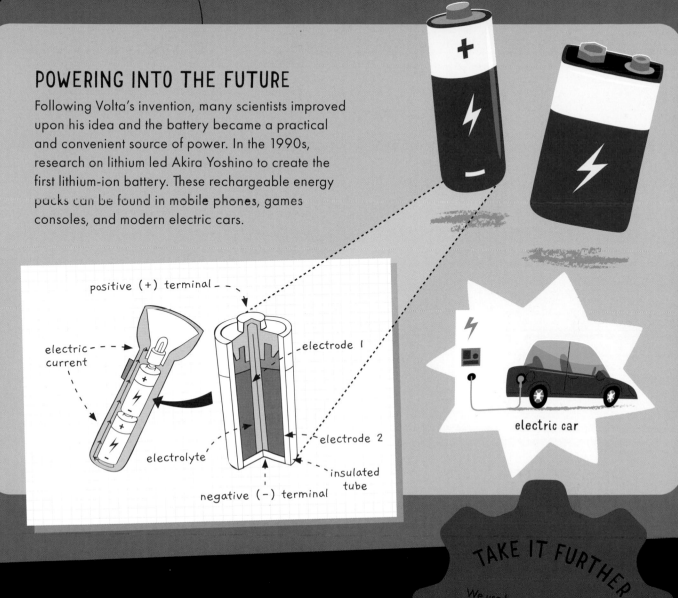

positive (+) terminal

electric current

electrode 1

electrolyte

electrode 2

negative (−) terminal

insulated tube

electric car

TAKE IT FURTHER

We use batteries in lots of different items around our homes.

How many things do you use that have batteries inside?

1948 −

Akira Yoshino
Kawasaki, Japan

Yoshino developed a battery that could be easily produced.

CODED COMMUNICATION

Until the early part of the nineteenth century, communicating with someone far away could take a very long time. Letters could take days, or even weeks, to reach their destinations.

In 1836, an American painter named Samuel Morse learned that it was possible to send electrical signals along a wire. He worked with Alfred Vail to create a **transmitter** that sent electrical pulses to a **receiver**. Morse invented a code of short dots and longer dashes to represent numbers. Vail expanded this to include letters and punctuation marks.

Morse and Vail's Morse key - - - -

1763 - 1805

Claude Chappe
Brûlon, France

Chappe's system, semaphore, needed people to use telescopes to read the signals and was quite slow.

1791 - 1872

Samuel Morse
New York, USA

Morse worked with Alfred Vail to create messages that could be received just seconds after they were sent.

WORKING WITHOUT WIRES

Developments in radio technology meant that, from the end of the nineteenth century, Morse code messages could be sent along **radio waves** instead of through wires. Guglielmo Marconi invented a radio that could transmit Morse code messages across long distances. This wireless communication was cheaper and meant that messages could be sent to ships that had no way to connect to electrograph wires.

EARLY TELEGRAPHY

Methods of communicating with drumbeats, smoke, flags or lit beacons have been around for a very long time. Visual signals are called "optical telegraphy" and, in the 1790s, the Chappe brothers invented semaphore telegraphs by using rotating arms that could be moved into different positions. These were positioned on the top of towers around 15 miles apart and operators translated the message from one tower before sending it on to the next. Claude Chappe named this "semaphore."

Chappe semaphore tower

1874 – 1937

Guglielmo Marconi
Bologna, Italy

In the mid-1890s, Marconi developed a practical radio device that that amateur radio enthusiasts still use today.

FUN FACT "Telegraph" means "to write at a distance"

TAKE IT FURTHER

Can you send a Morse code message or create your own code that could be used to write a message?

IN THE MIND OF A MACHINE

Alan Turing was a mathematician who worked on machines to crack codes during the Second World War. In 1950, he wrote that computers could use information to learn how to solve problems and make decisions. A few years later this **theory** was given the name "Artificial Intelligence" (AI) and the idea has been explored by computer scientists ever since.

WHAT IS THE TURING TEST?

Turing proposed a simple test to check the intelligence of a machine. In this test, a machine and a person are asked questions by someone who doesn't know which is which. If it is impossible to tell from their answers which one is the machine, it must be as intelligent as a person. Turing predicted that the test would be passed before the year 2000. No computer has passed the Turing Test conclusively ... yet!

FUN FACT In 1846, a mathematician named Charles Babbage came up with the idea for a machine that could play noughts-and-crosses.

1912 – 1954

Alan Turing
Manchester, England

At the heart of Turing's theory is the idea that computers could learn to think for themselves.

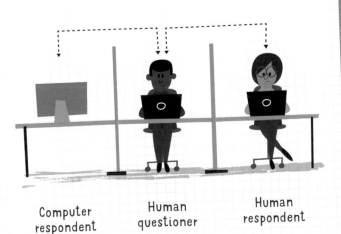

Computer respondent   Human questioner   Human respondent

MAN VS MACHINE

Since Turing's original idea, the technology of AI has continued to be developed and tested. In the 1990s, a company called IBM built Deep Blue, a computer that was **programmed** to play chess. The ultimate test for this piece of AI was to play against the chess grandmaster and champion Garry Kasparov. In February 1996, Kasparov and Deep Blue played six games of chess. Deep Blue won the first game but Kasparov won three and the final two were draws. Kasparov was the clear winner but there was a rematch just over a year later.
This time Deep Blue won!

TAKE IT FURTHER

Artificial Intelligence is created by computer programmers.

Do you think this means that they can have human prejudices and flaws?

Since the early 2010s, AI technology has found its way into ordinary homes as digital assistants that can recognize voice commands and carry out different activities.

1995–1997

Deep Blue
New York, USA

Deep Blue was a great example of AI. Deep Blue was retired in 1997 and parts of it are now in museums.

2000s

Digital assistants change the way we live.

FASCINATING FASTENINGS

Clothes fastenings have taken many forms over thousands of years. From brooches to laces to buttons and hooks, many of them are tricky and can take time to fasten.

In 1851, an engineer called Elias Howe invented an "Automatic, Continuous Clothing Closure." This early version of the zipper was never introduced to a wide market but, forty years later, Whitcomb L. Judson created a "clasp locker." This was a guide that connected a chain of metal hooks on boots and shoes. He followed this idea with a row of hooks that were pulled together called the "c-curity." It was unsuccessful because the fastening kept bursting open.

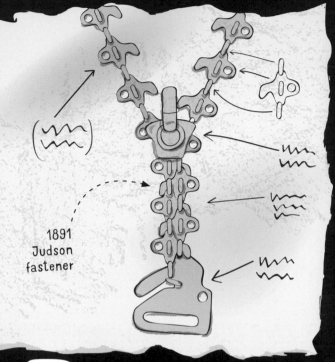

1891 Judson fastener

FROM HOOKS TO TEETH

Judson started The Universal Fastener Company and, in 1906, the company hired a Swedish engineer named Gideon Sundback. He replaced the hooks with tiny spoon-shaped rows of metal that locked together. His invention was secure and flexible, which meant that it could be used in all kinds of clothing. The company was renamed The Hookless Fastener Company.

Hook fastening zip

In 1917, the fasteners were put into money belts that became popular with the US Navy because there were no pockets on their uniforms. They soon replaced buttons on the Navy's full-body outfits called jumpsuits.

FUN FACT The world's longest zipper is 3.1 miles (4.9 kilometers) long.

1843 – 1909

Whitcomb L. Judson
Chicago, Illinois, USA

Judson showed his invention at the World's Fair in Chicago in 1893.

1880 – 1954

Gideon Sundback
Hoboken, New Jersey, USA

Sundback improved on Judson's idea.

After the First World War, the hookless fastener continued to be used and, in the 1920s, the B. F. Goodrich Company put them into their rubber boots. At the time, the word "zip" meant "move rapidly." It also sounded like the noise the hookless fastener made so the boots were named the "Zipper." Soon after they were added into children's clothes and, when they could open at both ends, they were perfect for jackets.

TAKE IT FURTHER

Think about the zips that you use. Are they on your clothes? Your backpack? Your shoes?

What are they made from?

What makes them better than other kinds of fastening such as buttons?

FUN FACT Surgical zippers use zip technology to close and protect wounds.

GLOSSARY

Adzes
an ancient and versatile cutting tool, similar to an axe.

Archaeological evidence
the physical objects and remains left by humans throughout history.

Chemical energy
the energy that hold atoms and molecules together. It is released when a chemical reaction takes place.

Diode
an electrical component that only allows an electrical current to flow in one direction.

Dissected
something that has been cut apart in order to be examined in detail.

Electrical energy
the power that is produced when electrons move from one atom to another.

Electrode
conductor used to make contact with a non-metallic part of a circuit.

Electron
a negatively charged subatomic particle that is found in the nucleus of an atom.

Eurasian Steppe
a huge belt of grassland that stretches from eastern Europe to China.

Feng Shui
the ancient Chinese practice of arranging furniture in order to create a balanced and harmonious environment.

Filament
a fine wire inside a lightbulb that glows when an electrical current passes through it.

Geodetic
the science of geodesy which accurately measures the Earth's shape, gravity and orientation in space.

Hominid
a member of the group of modern and extinct great apes that includes humans, gorillas, orangutans and all their ancestors.

Incandescent light
light produced when a wire (filament) is heated by an electric current.

Lead alloy
formed when lead is combined with another metal in order to give it different properties.

Magnetized
something that has been turned into a magnet.

Magnetic North Pole
the place in the northern hemisphere that compass needles point to.

Mechanism
a mechanical device for doing something. It usually refers to the parts inside a machine.

Metallurgy
the study of metals and experimenting with their various properties.

Microchip

a collection of electronic parts, including transistors, on a tiny piece of semiconductor material. This material is usually a chemical element called silicon.

Moveable type

the separate parts of a printing press with the letters on them so that they can be moved around to make different words.

Packet-switching

when small pieces of data travel quickly and efficiently through computer networks before being put back together.

Pneumatic

when compressed air is used to make something move.

Programmed

when a computer has been given the instructions to carry out specific tasks.

Protocols

a set of rules for transmitting data between computer devices.

Radio wave

a type of electromagnetic radiation with the longest wavelength.

Receiver

a device that receives electrical signals.

Rim

the outer part of a wheel.

Semiconductor

a substance that enables the control of the flow of electric current. They are commonly used in electronic devices.

Spoke

Spokes are thin rods that connect the centre (hub) of the wheel with the outer edge (rim).

Spread spectrum

a type of wireless communication which sends a message across a wide range of frequencies. This makes it more secure and reduces interference.

Theory

A theory is an idea or set of ideas based on scientific evidence that explains how something works.

Tissue

a group of cells that have similar structures and functions.

Transistor

a semiconductor device that can amplify or switch electronic signals.

Transmitter

a device that sends out radio signals.

Vibrating

when something moves rapidly back and forth.

Vulcanized

treated with chemicals and heat to make it stronger and harder.

TAKE IT FURTHER

Technology is when scientific knowledge is used to create something practical. And it's everywhere! From the wheels on a bike to the cameras in mobile phones, technology has changed the entire world. It has made it easier to communicate with each other, it has helped us to see in the dark and it has given us the tools to find our way when we are lost.

The brilliant inventors in the pages of this book have created things that we take for granted but that we often don't stop to think about. <u>Which one was your favorite?</u>

How do you use technology? What are the things that you do in a day that use technological inventions? Here are some examples:

- You read printed words in your books.
- There's a zip on your coat.
- Maybe you have batteries in your toothbrush.

The future of technology is full of exciting new ideas. It is already allowing us to explore the universe. It is helping to protect the environment. It is changing medical treatments. But what will be next?

What do you think the future holds? Can you invent something yourself? Your idea could be silly or helpful. It could be simple or complex. What is the one thing you think that technology could improve, and why?

Something you invent could have the power to make the world a better place and to change the way we work together.

<u>The possibilities are endless!</u>